Meditation

Effortless Meditation Techniques and Activities to Attain Freedom from Stress and Anxiety

(Effective Strategies for Managing Anger and Controlling Sexual Desires)

Bogdan Ibragimova

TABLE OF CONTENT

How Meditation Works 1

Meditating While Maintaining Focused Attention On A Visual Representation. 11

Get Started With Meditation 35

Develop Mindfulness Of The Current Moment. 43

Important Components Of Meditation 53

Exercises For Mindfulness In Meditation 69

Stress And Ill Health 82

The Role Of Meditation In Mitigating Pain And Alleviating Symptoms Of Depression 100

An Analysis Of The Desired Future Outlook 106

An Analysis Of The Distinctions Between Hypnosis And Relaxation Techniques 112

What 5-Minute Meditations Are 120

Enhancing Critical Thinking Skills: A Guide To Amplifying Your Analytical Abilities 150

How Meditation Works

The objective of meditation is to cultivate equilibrium among the cognitive faculties, affective states, and physiological well-being.

For countless centuries, the Eastern hemisphere has possessed extensive knowledge regarding the profound advantages derived from the practice of meditation. Ultimately, in the preceding century, the Western hemisphere has not merely grasped this phenomenon, but has fervently delved into the examination of its underlying principles and mechanics.

Extensive evidence has repeatedly demonstrated that mental stress serves as both a catalyst and underlying factor for numerous physiological afflictions. To cultivate a semblance of control over our physical well-being, it is imperative that we first establish a sense of command over our mental well-being.

The utilization of meditation for alleviating anxiety, depression, and stress is steadily on the rise. This phenomenon is exerting a ripple effect on our physical well-being, contributing to the alleviation of ailments such as persistent pain, cardiovascular ailments, gastrointestinal disorders, hypertension, cognitive impairments, and enhanced immunological resilience.

It has additionally demonstrated efficacy in facilitating the management of nicotine, substance, and alcohol dependencies.

However, how can the act of calmly sitting for a duration of 15 to 30 minutes daily possibly accomplish these profound outcomes?

AND

Is it possible to derive benefits from initial stages of meditation, or is it a prerequisite to engage in months of practice before witnessing any enhancements?

Meditation facilitates the tranquility of our mind, enabling detachment from the routines of everyday existence. It channels our prana, or vital life force, and directs it inwardly, enabling a seamless and unobstructed flow through our Chakra system.

According to the esteemed Dr. Ron Alexander, a distinguished psychotherapist, the Director of The Open Mind Training Institute located in California, and an accomplished author of the renowned publication Wise Mind Open Mind, it has been proposed that the human brain can be classified into five distinct categories of cognitive activity.

The Gamma State:

Gamma is characterized by heightened brain activity and enhanced cognitive receptivity. It represents a degree of excessive activity that, when exposed to an excess of stimulation, can elicit sensations of anxiety.

The Beta State:

This state of mind is widely prevalent. The cognitive state facilitates our ability to strategize, exert effort, evaluate, and resolve issues.

The Alpha State:

This is the state of ease and tranquility where one can delight in the present, derive pleasure from their surroundings, experience sensations of joy, and attain a serene level of consciousness.

The Theta State:

The mental state that is attained during the practice of meditation. At this juncture, our conscious mind relinquishes its control and cedes authority to our unconscious mind. It is a sanctuary from the external disruptions of daily existence and the societal norms that dictate our actions. We possess a conscious understanding of our environment, yet we remain attuned to our innermost beings, harmonizing with the natural forces that surround us. In the Theta state, individuals have the capacity to tap into their intuition and experience heightened self-awareness.

The Delta State:

For the majority of individuals, this is a condition that can only be attained during the deepest stage of our sleep cycle. Individuals who have devoted their existence to the practice of meditation, such as the esteemed Buddhist Monks, possess the inherent capacity to effortlessly attain this state.

The sympathetic branch of the autonomic nervous system is responsible for eliciting the Fight or Flight response. It bears the responsibility for the disarray prevailing within our cognitive processes. Dr.

Herbert Benson, a respected professor of Mind & Body medicine at Harvard Medical School, has conducted a series of scientific inquiries focused on the practice of meditation. The researcher's results indicate that during a state of meditation, there is a shift in blood distribution from the sympathetic nervous system to the parasympathetic nervous system.

As a result, it induces a state of relaxation, decelerates our cardiac rhythm, and engenders a decreased demand for oxygen within the body. Furthermore, the substantial advantages we derive from engaging in daily meditative practice extend beyond heightened levels of consciousness.

Regular daily practice will prevent your stress levels from escalating to a degree that could induce illness. The enduring advantages shall not be immediately accomplished. Similar to any valuable pursuit, attaining the Theta state requires diligent effort and commitment.

Initially, you may encounter a tendency towards frequent distraction, yet consistent training will enhance your ability to concentrate. It is necessary to enhance the cognitive abilities of your mind, and through consistent practice, it will gradually become more effortless, reaching a stage where minimal conscious effort is required.

It is improbable that you will observe considerable advantages initially, while you are in the process of acquiring the ability to achieve a state of meditation. However, after consistently engaging in meditation on a daily basis for a few weeks, you ought to begin discerning a discernible improvement in both your physical and mental state.

With the passage of time, there will be a noticeable improvement as you further familiarize yourself with your inner being and address any physical disharmony that your body encounters.

"The advantages of engaging in daily meditation within the initial months are expected to encompass:

A more relaxed state

Better quality of sleep

Reduction of stress and alleviation of muscular tension

Increase in energy levels

Increased stamina

Certain regions of the body may undergo a reduction in pain.

A mind that exhibits heightened clarity and concentration.

Enhanced self-consciousness

Outlook is more optimistic

A prevailing sense of tranquility

Enhanced tolerance towards others.

"The enduring advantages of practicing meditation on a daily basis should encompass:

Improvements in overall health

Enhanced immune system efficiency resulting in reduced incidence of illness and expedited recuperation from ailments.

Circulation is improved

Pain is reduced

Improved social skills

Self-motivation is high

Memory and cognitive functions exhibit enhanced strength

Confidence increases

Deep recognition and understanding of your true self and the world around you

Strength of mind

Meditating While Maintaining Focused Attention On A Visual Representation.

1. Please refrain from initiating the development of this program until you have achieved mastery in program 5, specifically focusing on meditation.

2. As a subject of focused attention, one may opt for a design, geometric figure, character, and the like. The heightened focus of the image aids in the prevention of intrusive thoughts and alleviates feelings of distress.

3. Physical activity is conducted for a duration of 15 minutes per day, with a frequency of 5 to 7 days per week, spanning a period of two weeks. Subsequently, there is a likelihood of extending the duration to 30 minutes.

4. Contemplate a specific visual stimulus during a span of approximately one

month, and subsequently deliberate on the potential inclusion of this practice within your overall regimen of meditation.

5. Please append the specified exercise to the visual representation. Envision a vacant area situated atop your cranium. Please populate this area with the visual representation originating from your imagination. Contemplate this image using your abstract imagination. It is conceivable that you may have a preference for engaging in meditation while concurrently engaging in the process of visualizing, wherein you create and envision your own bespoke mental imagery during your personal meditation sessions. It is possible that the failure to complete this meditation session, during which you engage in a visualization exercise with your own image, could potentially lead to an inclination to depict it through drawing or painting. Within this context, the utilization of it can be

extended to subsequent instances of meditation as well.

PROGRAM 7 - Guided Meditation "Lotus Blossom of Infinite Petals".

In Eastern cultural traditions, the lotus flower, adorned with numerous petals, serves as a potent symbol denoting the interconnectedness of all phenomena and entities within the expansive universe.

1. Within a tranquil setting that you have carefully selected for the purpose of contemplation, assume the posture that you have developed proficiency in.

2. Please choose the word, image, or idea that serves as the focal point of the lotus. During the initial fortnight, it is advisable to employ vocabulary that conveys a positive connotation by utilizing terms

such as "happiness," "peace," and "friendship."

and so on. This will contribute to the establishment of a positive atmosphere.

3. Direct your attention solely to the designated word. Simultaneously, you will invariably encounter a number of connections emerging. Consider the potential of the power of association manifesting itself in a single word or concept, akin to a petal affixed to the core word. Take a moment, lasting roughly 7 seconds, to contemplate the intricacies of the relationship that exists between them. Do refrain from excessive enthusiasm in attempting to comprehend the significance of this communication. It might be immediately obvious to you, however, it could potentially induce perplexity. Regardless, retreat to the main path and await the subsequent connection.

4. Perform this exercise with regularity for approximately 10 minutes per day, over the course of a fortnight. Over the course of the upcoming three weeks, it is advised to augment the duration of the sessions to a span ranging between 20 and 30 minutes. Consequently, upon completion of this timeframe, it would be prudent to deliberate on the inclusion of this particular form of meditation within your routine regimen.

Additional remark. Please bear in mind that the objective of this particular method of meditation is the cultivation of self-discipline, as opposed to attaining "enlightenment." Engaging excessively with intriguing associations poses a significant hindrance to the successful practice of this form of meditation.

PROGRAM 8 - The Practice of External Observation in Meditation.

This exercise bears resemblances to the exercise titled "I understand," however, it diverges in that the latter incorporates visualization, involving the application of one's imagination. Certain individuals posit that the faculty of imagination has the capacity to promote the practice of meditation, while conversely, there are those who contend that it hinders the said endeavor. Individually ascertain the benefits this exercise yields for oneself.

1. In a tranquil setting of your choosing, assume the posture that you have perfected for the purpose of meditation.

2. Kindly shut your eyes and passively observe the uninterrupted stream of your thoughts, emotions, and physical sensations.

3. When one experiences a thought, feeling, or sensation, it is appropriate to articulate them by expressing them

through written words, emanating from a metaphorical cloud above one's head, as often depicted in literary illustrations.

4. Direct your attention to this image for a duration of 6 to 10 seconds, after which proceed to the subsequent frame. Please withhold judgment until you have beheld the ensuing "cloud" and proceed to replicate the aforementioned procedure. Please refrain from pondering the substance of the "cloud" but rather observe its appearance. It is conceivable that a repetitive occurrence of the identical term may transpire, and a number of the "small clusters" could potentially be devoid of substance. Please refrain from being bothered by it, as this is the way it is meant to be. Calmly observe imaginary clouds.

5. Engage in this exercise for a duration of 10 minutes daily, spanning 5 to 7 occurrences per week, over the course of several weeks. Upon the conclusion of this

designated period, you will possess the ability to ascertain the decision of whether or not to incorporate it within your meditation regimen.

The subsequent iteration of this exercise entails envisioning oneself positioned at the lowest point of a considerably profound basin replete with water. As thoughts, feelings, or sensations arise within your consciousness, envision them gradually ascending within air bubbles towards the water's surface, allowing this process to unfold for a duration of 6 to 10 seconds. After the dissipation of the bubble, please exercise patience until the subsequent one emerges.

The third alternative for this exercise: Certain individuals harbor a degree of aversion towards envisioning themselves immersed underwater while the emergence of "clouds" from their head elicits a sense of unease. If you belong to this group, you can envision yourself stationed at the riverside, observing the log as it drifts downstream at a leisurely pace. For a duration of approximately 6-10 seconds, diligently observe how the log hovers within your line of sight, in tandem with any cognitive reflections, sensory perceptions, or emotive experiences, until the log eventually dissipates from your visual perception. Please resume the vigilance of the river in expectation of the arrival of the log containing the novel concept.

The fourth alternative for this exercise entails visualizing your thoughts ascending in a billowing haze emanating from the flames.

Requesting Consciousness When Forgiveness Is Required

Grant us absolution for our monetary obligations, just as we bestow forgiveness upon those who are indebted to us.

Matthew 6:12 KJV

This leads us to the subsequent issue, obstacle, prospect, or extraordinary occurrence. We must exert equal effort in extending forgiveness for the debts of others, as we do when seeking forgiveness for our own debts. When we convey or express detrimental words, thoughts, or actions towards others, we incur a moral obligation upon ourselves.

We must practice forgiveness. It may present a challenging endeavor. Forgiveness necessitates both compassion and empathy. We ought to engage in introspection and examine our own actions towards those who have legitimate reasons to seek retribution from us. To attain forgiveness, it is imperative that we extend forgiveness unto others. In times of anger, engage in the practice of meditation and introspection by inquiring, "What is the significance of this emotion?" Have I reciprocated these actions toward someone else? Be honest with yourself. Remain calm and refrain from passing judgment or suppressing your thoughts.

The "12 Steps of Alcoholics Anonymous" entails conducting a thorough examination of one's moral conscience and subsequently seeking to rectify any wrongs committed. When malevolent or incorrect thoughts arise within our minds, and we feel the urge to seek retribution, pass judgment, or entertain thoughts of harm, it is imperative that we promptly redirect our thinking towards the concept of forgiveness. Peter asked Jesus, "Lord, if my brother keeps on sinning against me, how many times do I have to forgive him? "Sevenfold?" "No, not merely sevenfold," replied Jesus, "but rather seventyfold, for the Kingdom of Heaven resembles this" (Matthew 18:21-22 GNT).

Jesus provided a demonstration of the unyielding borrower who failed to exhibit compassion despite holding the capacity to do so. To prevent the accumulation of debts, it is imperative to extend forgiveness in advance, thus avoiding the allure of temptation (Matthew 18:23-35). This liberates us from malevolence. The Divine Spirit aids us in comprehending our impending actions and the financial liability we are about to incur.

In order for divine inspiration to manifest within us, it is imperative that we extend forgiveness. This will enable us to tap into our inner reservoirs of creativity, enabling us to effectively address issues, surmount obstacles, and seize prospects that arise while navigating the complexities of life. I acknowledge that accepting this reality may be difficult. A particular individual purportedly made the assertion, "If I possess the ability to regulate your emotions, I shall possess dominion over you." Forgiveness, on the other hand, entails abstaining from granting authority to external entities such as other individuals, social media, or divergent ideologies in determining one's actions and behavior towards benevolence and humanitarian endeavors.

Another crucial aspect is acquiring the ability to absolve ourselves by resolving our own feelings of guilt and embracing the forgiveness bestowed upon us by the divine. What feelings of guilt are you presently clinging to? What culpability is obstructing your ability to attain inner tranquility?

Guilt pertains to an action, conduct, utterance, contemplation, or undertaking. Individuals possess the ability to exert influence over us through the manipulation of guilt, particularly within religious institutions. Undoubtedly, "the system" carries out this task. Nevertheless, in order to emancipate ourselves, we must exhibit the virtue of forgiveness and embrace the act of being forgiven. This can assist us in alleviating the detrimental effects of anger and depression, which can ultimately result in mortal consequences.

We can be creative. Instead of constructing the dreams of individuals who may not prioritize our best interests, we have the capacity to establish our communities and pursue our own aspirations. According to the passage in Proverbs 29:18 from the New International Version (NIV), it states that in the absence of divine guidance or revelation, individuals tend to abandon self-discipline and moral boundaries. While engaged in the practice of meditation, the Holy Spirit enables individuals to experience a divine revelation, enabling them to attain a heightened understanding of a more comprehensive perspective that extends beyond superficiality.

The clarity of the Hermetic Principle of Cause and Effect is evident. In order to obtain forgiveness, it is necessary for one to extend forgiveness oneself. If you wish to avoid incurring financial obligations and/or seek absolution from any existing debts, it is imperative to extend forgiveness towards the debts owed to you by others. One will eventually experience the consequences of their own actions. Nothing happens by chance. There are individuals who address this matter by adopting the concept of reincarnation, which can be interpreted in various ways.

Within the context of Christian doctrine, it is stated that Jesus posed the following inquiry: "By whom are individuals proclaiming me to be?" (Matthew 16:13; Mark 8:27; Luke 9:18, KJV). The disciples offered a response by listing individuals who had passed away and were no longer living.

The Old Testament contains passages that discuss the intergenerational consequences wherein the transgressions committed by one generation become intertwined with the subsequent generations' retributions. The narrative of Adam's descent is interrelated with the principle of causality.

We must delve deeper into the matter. Numerous individuals engage in therapeutic endeavors, unraveling layers of their experience in pursuit of uncovering and discerning the underlying origins of their concerns. This aspect of prayer is intricately linked to the second chakra, known as the Sacral chakra, which governs our emotional realm encompassing both our sensory experiences and subsequent reactions to them. An individual posited that, "It is not the linguistic expression itself that leads to our downfall; rather, it is the recollection of the emotions intertwined with and enveloping that particular expression during the occurrence of the event that causes our downfall." Conversely, one might assert that it is not the lexical choice that sparks our creativity, but rather the emotions associated with and encompassing said choice that elevate us.

We all have sinned. Remorse is a vital remedy for granting forgiveness. It is imperative for us to acknowledge the fact that events occur and we frequently lack the awareness to perceive the comprehensive implications of our actions. The healing process is facilitated through the utilization of the sixth chakra, commonly referred to as the Third Eye, in conjunction with the emanation of love from the fourth chakra, known as the Heart. The wisdom acquired from our personal experience of seeking forgiveness enables us to extend forgiveness towards others. The Holy Spirit assists us in recognizing the detrimental consequences we inflict upon ourselves by withholding forgiveness.

Number three: Zen meditation.

Zazen, which is also known as Zen meditation, encompasses a form of contemplative practice centered around open-monitoring meditation. Open monitoring meditation pertains to the diverse array of meditative practices that involve cultivating a receptive awareness of one's internal state, characterized by observing and acknowledging one's mental and present-moment experiences.

In contrast to breath mindfulness and body scan meditations, this particular form of meditation does not require concentrated focus or attentiveness towards a singular object or sensation. Rather, it entails cultivating a comprehensive state of general awareness encompassing both the physical and non-physical dimensions of existence.

Zen meditation confers considerable advantages. As an illustration, due to its emphasis on open awareness, it possesses the capacity to cultivate discernment, tranquility of the mind and body, and the aptitude to maintain focus on the breath—thus enhancing the ability to observe thoughts as they surface and impartially allow them to dissipate.

How to

"Presented below is a step-by-step guide on how to engage in the practice of zazen meditation:

Step 1

Enter a serene environment conducive to contemplation. Upon entering this area, assume a posture that allows for proper sitting; traditionally, zazen is performed in a seated position, but feel free to choose the posture that provides maximum comfort and alignment for you.

In this particular form of meditation, the objective is to assume a meditative posture that facilitates the stillness of the body, enabling the mind and body to attain a harmonious state of tranquility and interconnectedness. During the course of your meditation practice, endeavor to maintain a state of complete stillness throughout its duration.

Zazen places particular emphasis on posture, whereby one must ensure that the spine remains erect yet relaxed, shoulders are retracted, head maintains a neutral position with the chin tucked in, and hands rest comfortably, while the gaze is directed downward at a 45-degree angle.

In assuming this posture, establish a pensive look and redirect your complete cognitive focus to the breath, inhaling and exhaling through either the mouth or the nostrils, according to your preference for comfort. Similar to the mindfulness breath meditation approach, endeavor to perceive the breath and fully engage with it as though observing it with fresh eyes for the initial occasion; meditation entails a mindful inquisitiveness directed towards a singular focus.

Step 2

In the practice of Zazen meditation, the breathing serves as a focal point. To cultivate focused attention and prevent the mind from engaging with extraneous thoughts, one must count the breath, designating the inhalation as one and the exhalation as two. Execute this action for a duration of ten iterations, and subsequently recommence the procedure. In the event that specific thoughts divert your mindful focus, recognize this occurrence—initially, it may require some time to observe when the mind has strayed—and subsequently resume the enumeration from the point at which you had discontinued.

Step 3

Engaging in the practice of breath meditation as delineated previously will result in attaining a heightened level of serenity and groundedness. Once you experience this state, which may require a significant duration of time or even multiple sessions of breath mindfulness meditation, transition to the practice of open monitoring of your internal mental state. Adopt an attitude of detached and nonjudgmental observation, akin to that of an impartial observer, as you monitor your thoughts.

Zazen meditation proves particularly efficacious as a means of alleviating stress and anxiety due to its inherent capacity for facilitating heightened awareness of one's breath and the diligent observation of thoughts as they emerge and dissipate. Consequentially, individuals are better equipped to discern worrisome thoughts, including repetitive negative thoughts, which persist beyond acknowledgment and subsequent detachment from conscious observation.

Engaging in cognitive processes is not inherently negative; on the contrary, engaging in the process of cognition, specifically observing the presence and passage of thoughts, while maintaining conscious awareness of the predominant thoughts, aids in the development of open monitoring awareness. This form of awareness enables individuals to consciously perceive their own physical, mental, and emotional states, thereby promoting emotional resilience.

Having a conscious state of mind will enable you to engage in what experienced meditators refer to as "the capacity to observe one's thoughts." This essentially entails the ability to observe the arrival and departure of thoughts, and to fully reside in and be completely conscious of the current moment, or the PRESENT.

Get Started With Meditation

After extensively exploring the concept of meditation and its significance in our lives, we shall now proceed to delve into the process of initiating meditation. Please bear in mind that meditation is a straightforward practice that does not necessitate any extravagant efforts on your part. It pertains to achieving a state of relaxation in both your physical body and mental faculties. So let's get started.

Select a suitable time period

I feel compelled to bring this matter to your attention because it is widely believed that engaging in meditation during a specific hour of the day can yield the highest potential benefits. Wrong, absolutely wrong. Meditation solely constitutes a practice of relaxation, and should one find oneself occupied or mentally preoccupied during the appointed time, the pursuit of meditation becomes rendered inconsequential. The practice of meditation is best undertaken at a mutually agreeable time, wherein one is least susceptible to disruptions or intrusions.

In my personal opinion, I find the time of sunrise and sunset to be the most optimal for engaging in meditation. During these hours, the surrounding environment exudes a sense of tranquility and serenity, thereby enabling one to fully maximize their meditation experience. Nevertheless, as previously mentioned, meditation can be practiced at any given time throughout the day, provided that this time is dedicated solely and exclusively to achieving a state of relaxation and engaging in meditation.

Select a tranquil location for engaging in the practice of meditation.

Just as the selection of an appropriate hour is essential for engaging in meditation, likewise the choice of location holds equal significance for undertaking this practice. This is precisely why I have a preference for engaging in meditation during the early morning or evening hours - due to the tranquility that prevails during these times. Therefore, you can effortlessly attain a state of relaxation and, as a result, derive optimal advantages from engaging in meditation.

I recommend engaging in meditative practices within the confines of your private garden or a nearby public park, as the surrounding environment greatly facilitates an optimal meditative experience. If the option of visiting a park or having a garden within your property is financially unfeasible or non-existent, the terrace of your residence can serve as an equally enjoyable alternative. It is recommended that the meditation area be located in an open-air setting, as the calming presence of nature is undeniably one of the most profoundly soothing experiences one can encounter.

Assume a relaxed bodily position.

After establishing the location and time for your meditation practice, proceed to assume a comfortable bodily position. However, it is important not to simply use a pillow for back support and deceive oneself into thinking that one is engaging in proper meditation. Such an approach is not effective. Contrary to popular belief, it is not necessary to assume the Padmasana (lotus-position) in order to engage in the practice of meditation. Therefore, it is imperative to maintain a state of relaxation in the positioning of your head, neck, shoulders, and all other bodily components, while also remaining adaptable with your overall posture. During the meditation practice, it is advisable to keep your eyes closed and maintain an upright posture with a straight spine.

If you adhere to these instructions, you are effectively practicing meditation. Please proceed with reading the subsequent points.

It is advisable to engage in a brief period of deep breathing prior to commencing the practice of meditation.

Engaging in a few moments of deep breathing prior to commencing meditation can greatly benefit the body by facilitating a heightened state of relaxation. This would enable you to regulate your breathing rhythm and facilitate your body's transition into a state of calm and tranquil meditation. This constitutes a common knowledge that is widely recognized, yet regrettably lacks adherence by the majority. Therefore, I kindly request that you exercise sincere diligence in adhering to these instructions.

Engage in meditation on a stomach that is minimally occupied.

Engaging in meditation immediately after meal consumption may lead to unintended drowsiness and potential for falling asleep. Therefore, it is advised to refrain from meditating immediately after eating. An optimal period for engaging in meditation would range from approximately four hours prior to consuming a meal to a minimum of 3-4 hours following the conclusion of a meal. This does not apply during this interval. Additionally, I would advise against engaging in meditation on an entirely empty stomach, as this can induce feelings of hunger and impede one's ability to focus on achieving a state of relaxation. Therefore, it is advisable to abstain from excessive eating and engage in meditation while in a state of moderate satiation to optimize the outcome.

Lastly, endeavor to maintain a calm composure.

Engaging in the practice of meditation, as previously discussed, primarily involves achieving a state of relaxation for both the mind and body. Additionally, considering that you have selected a time slot that accommodates your schedule and entails no conflicting obligations, there appears to be no necessity for you to hasten through the task. This phenomenon is observed in a multitude of individuals. They consistently exhibit a sense of haste when engaging in their meditation routine, swiftly progressing to their subsequent tasks.

The primary objective of engaging in meditation is to disrupt the perpetual and uninterrupted labor that imposes a strain on one's mental and physical well-being. If you were to incorporate meditation into your daily routine, it is likely that you will experience an increase in your workload, consequently leading to heightened levels of suffering. Meditation is intended for the purpose of promoting relaxation, and it ought to be maintained as such. Even a brief session of meditation, lasting 10 to 15 minutes, requires your mind to enter a state of complete relaxation, free from any distractions related to other tasks or responsibilities.

Furthermore, ensure that you refrain from hastily opening your eyes and departing. Gradually and delicately raise your eyelids in a slow manner. Through this practice, one gradually attains a heightened sense of awareness of their surroundings, fully realizing the intended goal of achieving a state of relaxation. Conversely, should one hasten through the practice, any benefits derived from meditation will be negated.

Develop Mindfulness Of The Current Moment.

Do you ever choose to solely focus on the present moment? Admittedly, life presents constant challenges, as we encounter daily uncertainties that lie beyond our sphere of influence. In certain circumstances, we are compelled to rely solely on the prospect of a favorable outcome.

However, this is not always the scenario. Occasionally, we find ourselves making unfavorable choices, encountering individuals unsuited for us, and, unfortunately, being exposed to unpleasant circumstances. This discourages us from reflecting on a past fraught with acts of betrayal, failures, and challenges. When the past lacks reminiscence, the future becomes our sole focus. Nonetheless, the future remains equally bleak. We do not possess the ability to predict future outcomes and the occurrence of favorable circumstances is uncertain to us. In light of the unpredictability of the past and future, we possess the present moment.

In this particular instance, the matter at hand revolves around making a deliberate decision to relinquish attachment to both past occurrences and future prospects, while directing one's attention solely towards the present moment. By adhering to this approach, one will attain a state of tranquility, serenity, and soundness of mind.

Utilizing mindfulness techniques, one can effortlessly incorporate present moment meditation into their daily routine at any given time. It constitutes one of the forms of meditation that can facilitate a comprehensive resolution of depression and anxiety. Through cultivating an awareness of the current moment and directing the entirety of your attention towards it, you instill within yourself a vigilant, serene, and lucid state of mind. Current moment meditation entails relinquishing all emotional agitation and inner mental dialogue, and attaining a state of emptiness. Through this void, individuals may attain a state of serene and profound tranquility.

Nevertheless, attaining this state of mind can prove to be a complex undertaking. This is specifically intended for individuals who are new to meditation. However, over time, individuals can develop the capacity to cultivate mental discipline and concentrate solely on a singular notion. This represents the current chronological instant. It is imperative to be mindful that the current moment remains concealed whenever our minds are driven by ego. The term "egoic mind" refers to the tendency to mentally project oneself into the future, fabricating illusions that instill a sense of impending failure and fixating on past setbacks. By directing your attention solely to the present moment, you transcend illusionary perceptions and detach yourself from the ego.

While considering the future or contemplating the past can yield positive outcomes, particularly if such reflections contribute to personal growth, any instance wherein these thoughts breed excessive concern, anxiety, uncertainty, or remorse will prove detrimental to your well-being.

Might we consider directing our attention towards the current instant?

The act of cultivating mindfulness involves harnessing one's existing self to foster an understanding of the current moment.

You can achieve complete presence in the current moment by engaging in any of the subsequent activities:

• Heighten your awareness of all visible, perceptible, audible, or aromatic stimuli

• Develop mindfulness of your breathing patterns. In this context, the alternative way to say it in a formal tone could be: "Here, emphasis will be placed on the respiratory process, the physiological and psychological transformations occurring in your body, and the kinematic aspects associated with your respiration."

• Begin to observe and connect with your physical sensations, delving beyond external awareness and exploring the internal realm of your body. To illustrate this point, take note of the sensation originating from your hands' innermost core.

• Heighten your spatial awareness

Setting up

When desiring to engage in the practice of present moment meditation, it is advisable to assume a posture that is affable, yet guarantees wakefulness. The optimal initial step revolves around fostering an atmosphere conducive to maintaining a vigilant mindset and a tranquil physique. If it is feasible to assume an upright position, it is advised to opt for that stance rather than reclining. As you make further advancements, you will gradually attain the proficiency to determine the optimal posture that suits you personally, as well as gain the ability to manipulate postures in order to evoke diverse emotional responses.

Transition from a cognitive state to one of sensory perception.

When cultivating mindfulness, endeavor to disengage from customary patterns of mental rumination. Strive to cultivate a heightened sense of mindfulness and embrace the richness of the current moment. In this particular instance, you will have the ability to regulate what enters, exits, and is to be closed off from your thoughts. One may also consider engaging in self-verbalization of their actions. As an illustration, when directing your undivided attention to the present moment, you may verbalize, "I am presently cultivating consciousness of the current instance and relinquishing attachments to both past experiences and the ambiguous future."

Awareness

Our minds possess an inherent inclination towards ceaseless contemplation. The optimal course of action would be to engage it with a mundane idea. Please bear in mind that initiating meditation can pose a significant challenge in terms of maintaining mental control. It will invariably necessitate a transition towards that which you do not desire. Hence, it is imperative to give utmost consideration to one's mental faculties. However, with the passage of time, it will become somewhat more manageable to concentrate.

To attain the state of mindfulness, redirect your focus:

• Upon detecting any apparent auditory signals, it is advisable to further focus one's attention in order to discern any underlying, more minute voices present in the ambient soundscape. Subtle auditory stimuli may encompass distant vehicular noises and the melodic chirping of birds. Continue to allow each sound to fade away while directing your attention towards any novel auditory stimuli.

- Be conscious of the sensations in your body; take notice of how your arms rest on your laps, the way your legs are interlocked, and the tactile experience of your clothes against your skin. Direct your attention towards any muscle experiencing tension, any sensations of pain, feelings of anxiety, or fluttering sensations occurring in the stomach region.

- Direct your attention towards regulating your breath. When attending to your breath, direct your attention towards both the exhaling and inhaling processes, as well as the coordinated movements of your bodily structures.

- Direct your attention to your thoughts. I have maintained a keen attentiveness to the emergence and swift passing of thoughts. Please ensure that you do not yield to the temptation of reacting, experiencing emotions, or passing judgment upon them; rather, simply allow them to pass. You will engage in the observance of your thoughts as they traverse, without any active intervention.

Similar to other forms of meditation, the practice of cultivating present moment awareness enables individuals to establish a profound connection with their true selves and the overarching reality, ultimately liberating oneself from the shackles of negativity. Additionally, you will have the capability to regulate the content that enters and exits your consciousness. The overarching objective of establishing this state is to enhance the depth of one's connection, to direct focus towards one's life, and to strive for the richness inherent in every individual moment. You will be acquiring the ability to liberate yourself, facilitating the infusion of vitality, joy, and contentment into your life.

Important Components Of Meditation

As previously indicated in Chapter 1, a multitude of meditation modalities can be observed; however, despite their inherent distinctions, the fundamental objective remains consistent across all, which is to cultivate an individual's consciousness, thereby enabling enhanced regulation and mastery over it. The following are several fundamental elements of meditation that are shared among various techniques:

-

Environment

-

Position

-

Relaxation

-

Meditation target

Each of these factors will contribute to enabling an individual to attain a meditative state. Prior to delving into a comprehensive examination of each of these points, it is beneficial to acquire a nuanced understanding of the nature of a meditative state.

A meditative state is a mental condition characterized by the following attributes:

-

Physique - motionless, at ease, tranquil, gentle respiration and pulse, possibly experiencing sensations of weightlessness.

-

Sensations - serene, poised, composed, aloof

-

Cognitive faculties - tranquil, easeful attentiveness, cognitively sound, observant, concentrated

-

Conduct - characterized by passivity, inactivity, deliberate movements performed at a leisurely pace

Meditation facilitates the attainment of a state of deep introspection. One can ascertain the correctness of their meditation practice by observing the aforementioned qualities within themselves.

Environment

It is possible to engage in the practice of meditation in any location, provided that one possesses the ability to filter out and ignore external disturbances. If you have not yet developed the habit, it is advisable to designate a space that is conducive to the practice of meditation.

"Some defining attributes of a meditation space include:

- Quiet and dimly-lit

- Pleasant

- Comfortable

- Safe

- Uncluttered

- With necessary items conveniently accessible

-

Decorated with meaningful images/objects

-

Equipped with articles conducive to inducing a state of trance, such as crystals, mandalas, incense, and gongs.

-

With minimal to nonexistent distractions

Establishing a designated space for meditation will facilitate the mental preparation necessary for achieving a meditative state with greater efficiency and ease. One may engage in meditation in their bedroom, library, place of worship, public park, or any location where tranquility and minimal disruption can be ensured. If possible, kindly affix a "do not disturb" sign outside the designated area or politely inform others to refrain from interrupting you during your meditative practice.

Position

Multiple meditative techniques necessitate the adoption of a specific posture. The majority of these methods revolve around maintaining an upright posture of the spine. It is widely held that when the spine maintains an upright position, the flow of energies coursing through it becomes less impeded. From a practical perspective, maintaining an upright posture effectively distributes the body's weight in a balanced manner, thereby reducing muscle tension.

There exist meditation techniques which require stillness, others that involve precise movements, and yet others where freedom of movement is allowed. Such practices as yoga, tai chi, and qi gong are characterized by the adoption of distinct bodily postures and movements. You are welcome to acquire this knowledge if you so desire; however, please be reminded that any posture or movement that aids in maintaining your focus will be suitable.

Outlined below are several conventional stances suitable for the practice of meditation:

- Assuming a seated position with an erect posture and ensuring that your feet are firmly planted on the ground.

- Assuming a seated position on the floor or a plush cushion with a preferable thickness ranging from 4 to 6 inches.

- Sitting crossed-legged

- Adopting a seated posture in the lotus or half-lotus position.

-

Assuming a reclined position (discouraged due to the potential of unintentionally dozing off)

-

Assuming a lateral position with the head supported by one arm.

You have the option to place your hands on your lap or knees, join them together in a prayerful gesture, engage in mudras (hand positions used in yoga), or alternatively, allow them to hang naturally by your sides.

The lotus position

"This particular posture is often regarded as a traditionally recognized stance for engaging in the practice of meditation:

1.

Assume a seated position on the ground and draw your left foot closer to your body. Place it gently on your right thigh, ensuring that the sole is facing upward.

2.

Raise your right lower limb and position it on your left upper limb, ensuring that the sole is oriented upward and the heel is in proximity to your abdominal region.

3.

It is imperative that your knees make contact with the floor.

4.

Maintain an upright posture: retract your shoulder blades and elevate your chest. Ensure that your chin remains in an aligned position with the horizontal plane.

5.

Place the tip of your tongue against the palatal region inside your mouth.

6.

Ensure that your mandible is in a relaxed position, allowing your maxillary and mandibular teeth to make gentle contact with one another.

The half lotus position

This posture bears resemblance to the full lotus pose, albeit with the notable distinction that only a singular sole of the foot faces upwards, while the other foot remains grounded on the floor. If the lotus position proves to be uncomfortable, please consider trying this alternative approach.

Relaxation

The inability to focus is inherent in instances when the body experiences tension and the mind is burdened. This predicament is addressed in numerous meditation practices through the inclusion of techniques that promote relaxation. The practice of meditation entails maintaining focused awareness, thereby necessitating a state of comfort that allows one to divert attention away from any extraneous distractions during the meditation session.

Please be mindful that relaxation should not be misconstrued as the act of dozing off. During the practice of meditation, it is crucial to acknowledge any instances of distraction or tension and consciously relinquish them, thereby maintaining a heightened state of awareness regarding one's actions. Nevertheless, you might consider practicing meditation as a means to facilitate a more effortless transition into sleep.

Physical Relaxation Exercise

Engaging in deliberate muscular contraction and subsequent relaxation elicits sensations of relaxation. Additionally, it is suggested that you engage in a cognitive examination of your body to identify any areas of muscular tension and subsequently alleviate it.

Contract or contractually tense each muscle group for a duration of 3 to 10 seconds, followed by subsequent relaxation. Experience the release of tension from the muscle. Additionally, one could induce an increase or decrease in the weight, temperature, or sensation of the body part to enhance the desired impact.

When initiating your practice, it can be beneficial to systematically address each muscle group in a consecutive manner, thereby honing the ability to perceive and alleviate any tension. One can commence by addressing the toes and feet, gradually ascending towards the head and face, or alternatively, by commencing with the head and face and working one's way downwards. Alternatively, one may also adhere to the following progression: hands, arms, and feet. Anterior and posterior aspects of the lower extremities, quadriceps and hamstrings, gluteal region, abdominal region, lumbar region, pectoral region, deltoids, cervical region, oral cavity and mandible, ocular region, and frontal and cranial areas.

Once you have grown accustomed to engaging in this progressive relaxation technique, you may opt to hasten the process. Allow your arms, legs, abdomen, chest, and subsequently the facial muscles to loosen and unwind. You may also choose to completely unwind your entire body simultaneously.

Mental Relaxation

Engaging in relaxation techniques can facilitate the calming of both body and mind. Chapter 3 delves into the discourse surrounding techniques for achieving mental relaxation.

Clothes

Should you wish to enhance your meditative state, you are welcome to don specialized clothing; however, any attire that is loose, lightweight, and comfortable will suffice. Ensure that your attire does not cause any distractions during the course of the session.

Meditation Target

The primary undertaking within the practice of meditation involves directing one's attention towards a singular objective or endeavor. This process aids in relinquishing the contents of your mind, leaving behind solely pure awareness. Prior to engaging in meditation, it is imperative to internally or vocally affirm that throughout the meditative process, all other matters hold no significance.

Please direct your full focus and attention towards:

- A mantra (chant)

- A word

- A sound
- An object
- A candle flame
- A mandala (symbolic art)
- An image
- An aspect of the wall
- An idea
- A holy person

- Your breath or heartbeat

It is essential to bear in mind that meditation centers around the practice of continually directing and redirecting one's attention. If you have lost your way, I kindly advise you to retrace your steps and return to your starting point. No criticisms necessary.

Having acquired the necessary knowledge on meditation, you are now prepared to commence your instruction on the practice. In the subsequent chapter, you will be instructed on a selection of conventional meditation practices that you can readily implement.

Exercises For Mindfulness In Meditation

As previously reiterated, there exists a myriad of approaches to engage in the practice of mindfulness meditation. Thus, I present to you several means by which you can integrate this remarkable technique into your daily routine.

Now you are equipped with the knowledge of various aspects on which to direct your attention during mindfulness meditation. You have demonstrated proficiency in assuming the appropriate positions. Consequently, it is opportune for us to delve into the various exercises at your disposal for your enjoyment.

Chocolate Meditation

Undoubtedly, this represents one of the most gratifying and delectable manifestations of mindfulness meditation. This would require approximately 5 to 15 minutes of your valuable time. You would require a single small square of chocolate. If you prioritize your health, we recommend opting for dark chocolate that boasts a substantial cocoa concentration. However, other variations of chocolate are also deemed acceptable.

To commence the meditation, adhere to the prescribed guidelines for posture, or alternatively, assume a restful and tranquil bodily position, ensuring the absence of extraneous thoughts from your mind. After you have prepared yourself, proceed to consume a portion of the chocolate square. Allow it to rest on the center of your tastebuds. Direct your attention to the cocoa's texture and its accompanying flavor. Please exercise caution and awareness of both the pleasant and unpleasant taste sensations present in the chocolate as you gradually consume liquefied fragments of it. Now that you have completely consumed that petite piece of chocolate, direct your focus towards the void that remains after the chocolate in your oral cavity. Gently elevate your hand while holding the remaining chocolate. Direct your focus towards the tactile sensations perceived between your digits, including the texture, cohesion, and adherence. Consume the final morsel of chocolate and focus your attention on the delightful flavor it presents. In the event that your thoughts veer off course, delicately guide them towards refocusing on the present moment.

As one navigates through the course of the day, in the event that feelings of stress or unease arise, it is recommended to revisit the emotions and contemplations elicited by this specific meditation.

Mantra Meditation

Through the mere experience of a single session of Mantra meditation, one is able to discern and experience the profound and beneficial impact it has specifically on alleviating stress. Through consistent practice, one shall observe a diminishing inclination towards reactivity in the face of distressing thoughts and emotions. In order to engage in this meditation, it is recommended that you allocate a minimum of 5 minutes from your schedule. Mantra meditation is particularly well-suited for individuals who struggle to attain mental tranquility, as it effectively addresses the persistent internal discourse that impedes their ability to achieve a state of cognitive emptiness. By adopting a mantra, one can effectively subdue the disruptive inner monologue.

Please ensure that you position yourself in a state of comfort. Establish a sense of calm and presence prior to commencing the practice of meditation. Eliminate any extraneous thoughts from your cognition and direct your attention solely towards the present moment. Prior to commencing your meditation practice, select a mantra. A mantra is a verbal expression, typically consisting of a phrase or word, which holds significance for individuals. It can range from a profound statement to a seemingly meaningless utterance like 'OM.' Simply select a mantra that feels comfortable and effortless for you to repeatedly recite. To begin the meditation, close your eyes, and say your mantra. Direct your attention solely towards the emotions, the auditory experience, and the repeated phrase, whilst disregarding any other distractions. In the event of any distractions, simply redirect your focus back to the mantra.

Walking Meditation

Given that mindfulness meditation involves engaging the mind, it follows that the body should not be restricted to a static posture. If you exhibit restlessness and experience enhanced concentration while in motion, a walking meditation proves to be an ideal practice for you. One can allocate a duration of 10 to 30 minutes daily for engaging in walking meditation. In addition to engaging in a beneficial physical workout, you are also engaging in a cognitive workout.

Before commencing the walking meditation, it is advisable to attire oneself in comfortable footwear and garments that would minimize potential distractions. Commence strolling at a leisurely gait. Initiate your contemplation by directing your attention towards your physical being. The experience of the sensation of walking, starting from your upper torso and extending all the way to the soles of your feet. Experience the motion of different muscular groups while engaging in ambulation. Once more, in the case of any distractions, kindly redirect your focus to the present moment.

Please be reminded that meditation may have numerous points of focus. One can alternatively focus their attention on the splendor of Mother Nature, particularly in the presence of picturesque surroundings. Additionally, one may direct their attention towards the ambient sounds produced by nature, such as the melodious songs of avian creatures. It is crucial to direct your mental attention towards the present moment and concentrate on the current situation. One's thoughts should refrain from transitioning abruptly and erratically between different subjects. In the event of such occurrence, gently redirect your cognitive focus towards the subject under consideration.

Loving – Kindness Meditation

This Mindfulness Meditation is widely renowned and highly favored among practitioners. The fundamental objective of this meditation practice revolves around directing kind and compassionate energy towards oneself or others. This would necessitate a minimum of 5 minutes of your valuable time.

Assume your position, adopt a state of relaxation in your body, and free your mind of any thoughts. Engage in a series of deliberate breaths to cultivate a serene state of mind and anchor yourself in the present. Initiate your meditation practice by cultivating self-love. Envision the depth of self-affection you possess. Express gratitude to yourself for the person you have become today, despite your weaknesses, flaws, and past mistakes—extend gratitude to yourself. Develop self-awareness and embrace your authentic self. Recite three or four affirming and optimistic statements inwardly, such as: may I experience mutual gratitude throughout the day; may I enjoy excellent physical condition, resilience, and serenity; may I be protected; may I attain contentment. If one desires personal growth, it is advisable to consider additional aspirations, such as cultivating a deeper sense of respect towards others, fostering greater diligence in one's endeavors, and so forth. Take pleasure in the sentiment of self-esteem and recognize the gratifying experience of embracing your own identity.

A noteworthy practical use of this form of mindfulness meditation is cultivating the ability to relinquish attachment. This proves particularly beneficial when dealing with individuals who are challenging. Therefore, rather than directing your attention inward, you can redirect all your compassionate and benevolent intentions towards that challenging individual. The process of forgiving may necessitate a significant investment of time and effort, yet eventually, it will facilitate your emotional healing and grant you access to the genuine advantages of releasing grudges.

Bath Meditation

Undoubtedly, this is one of the most calming methods of meditation. The combination of meditation and a warm bath offers transient alleviation of stress and fatigue in muscles. It is anticipated that this task will require a minimum of 15 minutes of your valuable time. In order to augment the tranquil ambience, it is recommended to utilize aromatherapy bath products, such as bath oils or bubble baths infused with the soothing aroma of lavender.

Prepare your bathtub and fill it with water heated to a comfortable temperature. Incorporate the requisite aromatherapy indulgence products that will be utilized. While engaging in this activity, it would be advantageous to begin mentally preparing yourself. This can be achieved by directing your attention towards the gentle sound of the flowing water or the pleasant aroma emanating from the bath. Opt for a focal point that brings sensory satisfaction. Once your bath is prepared, allocate a moment to collect your thoughts and ready yourself to center your attention on the invigorating force of warm water penetrating your fatigued and aching muscles. As you settle into the bath tub, assume a position that offers maximum comfort, taking care not to disrupt your contemplation of the soothing warmth. Take deliberate, unhurried breaths, focusing your attention on the rhythmic expansion and contraction of your abdomen as you inhale and exhale deeply. Direct your focus exclusively towards the present moment. Which aspect brings you the greatest satisfaction: the fragrance or the comforting heat of the water? Experience the alleviation of tension in your muscles as each inhalation and every passing moment immerses you in the comforting embrace of the heated bath.

Stress And Ill Health

When the stress response is protracted and there is a lack of physical intervention to alleviate the organism from this state, a multitude of unfavorable ramifications ensue. As an illustration, the fatty acids that are liberated into the circulatory system for the purpose of fueling the body are subsequently deposited along the arterial walls, culminating in the development of arteriosclerosis and eventual cardiac insufficiency. Elevated concentrations of hydrochloric acid in the gastric system can give rise to pronounced digestive discomfort, eventually culminating in the development of peptic ulcers. Unfortunately, due to space constraints within this book, it is not possible to delve further into the intricate details. However, it is scientifically established that stress holds significant recognition as the primary catalyst behind the development of hypertension, migraines, and insomnia. More importantly, it remains closely linked to various other maladies, with the most notable ones encompassing cancer, arthritis, and respiratory conditions including bronchitis and emphysema. However, the impact is not exhibited solely on a physical dimension. Neuropsychiatric conditions could arise, as well as maladaptive behaviors including substance misuse or criminal activities. The ramifications of this for society at large are readily apparent. At the individual level, it is well-known to anyone who has had the opportunity to reside or collaborate closely with individuals who bear immense burdens, as is the case for a majority of individuals, the considerable arduousness of such circumstances and the inherent susceptibility to their influence. Additionally, there has been the emergence of disconcerting evidence suggesting that expectant mothers facing prenatal stress may exert an influence on their infants, resulting in delayed development and heightened challenges in dealing with stressors and interpersonal tensions.

The range of stress-induced disorders is infinite. According to even the most cautious and traditionally inclined sources, a substantial majority of the ailments managed by primary care physicians can be attributed to psychosomatic factors or causes related to stress. According to certain projections, this statistic can reach up to 90 percent. Numerous healthcare professionals maintain the belief that prolonged stress can also induce heightened vulnerability to viral and other infections, which are conventionally classified as non-psychosomatic, by compromising the functionality of the immune system. Through the application of vaccination, antibiotics, and enhanced living standards, the eradication or containment of debilitating contagious illnesses such as smallpox, typhoid, cholera, and polio has been successfully achieved. However, it is notable that certain infectious diseases, like tuberculosis, have exhibited resistance to antibiotics, leading to a resurgence in their prevalence. Currently, in the more industrially advanced nations, cardiovascular disorders and cancer have emerged as the principal causes of mortality. These ailments, frequently referred to as maladies of modern society, exhibit a strong correlation with stress.

By adopting a cautious perspective on the influence of stress in the development of diseases and other types of negative health outcomes, it becomes evident that acquiring the skills to effectively manage stress is likely the most crucial measure an individual can undertake to promote favorable health and extend their lifespan. This statement does not imply that it is possible or advisable to entirely eradicate all forms of stress, nor does it insinuate that we should perpetually experience optimal health without exception. Episodes of sickness or emergencies can likewise serve as periods of profound individual metamorphosis, instigating highly favorable modifications in one's way of life and ideology. We must identify strategies to proactively mitigate stress before it escalates to hazardous thresholds. While vigorous physical activity may be deemed suitable by certain individuals, the majority of people are inclined to employ deliberate relaxation techniques that effectively deactivate the fight or flight response.

Meditation - inducing the state of relaxation through the activation of the relaxation response.

The physiological and biochemical adaptations that the body undergoes in reaction to stress are controlled by the two divisions of the autonomic nervous system - the sympathetic and the parasympathetic. The fight or flight response is a physiological reaction that arises from the activation of the sympathetic nervous system in response to an initial stress stimulus. Once the peril has subsided or the task has been successfully accomplished, the parasympathetic system is trigged, inducing a reaction that is diametrically opposed to the fight or flight response. The heart rate undergoes a decrease, leading to a reduction in blood pressure. Respiration becomes slower, resulting in a decreased intake of oxygen. The musculature experiences a state of relaxation, while the process of digestion persists.

As previously elucidated, protracted sympathetic arousal can give rise to severe health complications. Meditation counteracts this state of arousal by activating the parasympathetic response, which has also been termed 'the relaxation response'. Extensive research has been undertaken to investigate the impact of meditation, primarily focusing on the participation of renowned Zen masters, Indian yogis, and, in more recent times, Western individuals practicing Transcendental Meditation (TM). These studies have yielded evidence indicating that the practice of meditation is accompanied by:

- a notable reduction in heart rate accompanied by a decline or stabilization of blood pressure

- diminished respiration rate, superficial breathing, and decreased oxygen utilization

- A decline in skin conductance related to the attenuation of anxiety levels (during periods of anxiety or nervousness, individuals tend to experience increased sweating, leading to a decrease in skin resistance towards an electric current). Machines specifically engineered to assess electrical resistance can detect even the subtlest perspiration increments that remain imperceptible to the unaided human eye, thus forming the fundamental basis for lie detection.

- alterations in brainwave patterns suggestive of a state of calm attentiveness.

Meditation may be employed with the purpose of deactivating the fight or flight response. It is important to acknowledge that although the majority of meditation practices, including those outlined in this book, promote relaxation, certain methodologies employed in specific systems such as kundalini yoga may elicit heightened levels of alertness. It is worth noting that meditation's advantages transcend the duration of the practice itself, extending into the remaining hours of the day. Consequently, regular practitioners are better equipped to effectively manage the demands of their daily routines.

Physiological stimulation and recuperation among practitioners of meditation

Based on these findings, one could initially deduce that meditation results in reduced reactivity and increased non-responsiveness. This would, undoubtedly, be highly undesirable for a multitude of distinct reasons. To begin, it is important to note that physiological arousal plays a crucial role in situations that pose a risk, as it enables individuals to react promptly. Additionally, the conventional objectives of meditation encompass heightened sensitivity and perception rather than apathy and inaction.

Due to the necessity of research personnel and the utilization of measuring apparatuses, obtaining data on the performance of individuals practicing meditation in real-world scenarios is exceedingly challenging. Nevertheless, there exists supported evidence indicating that individuals who practice meditation indeed encounter heightened states of arousal as relevant. In a conducted study, a cohort comprising proficient practitioners of meditation, alongside a control group, were subjected to a profoundly distressing cinematic presentation. This particular film, initially designed to emphasize the significance of adhering to safety protocols among carpenters, was employed for the purpose of this study. The movie portrays three incidents, one resulting in fatality, which occurred due to the disregard of these protocols. As anticipated, there was a direct correlation between the incidents portrayed in the film and the fluctuations observed in both groups, indicating an increase and decrease in skin conductivity and heart rate, respectively. However, the outcome that proved to be the most captivating was completely unforeseen. The participants who engaged in meditation demonstrated markedly higher levels of skin conductivity and heart rate immediately prior to each stressful event, yet they also exhibited a notably expedited recuperation afterwards. This implies that individuals who engage in meditation possess a broader spectrum of reaction compared to those who do not practice meditation, and exhibit heightened perceptiveness.

Acclimation to recurrent or persistent stress stimuli

Connected to this pattern of arousal and subsequent recuperation is the phenomenon commonly referred to as habituation. If a person is exposed to a recurring or disputatious circumstance, such as severe overpopulation or a noxious noise caused by a road drill, the physiological stress reaction will gradually abate. This capacity to adapt to recurrent and inevitable stimuli in the surrounding milieu is imperative. The failure to accomplish this results in stress-related conditions. Furthermore, based on empirical data, the outcomes of various experiments conducted on proficient meditators and control groups, who were exposed to prolonged or repetitive unpleasant sounds, reveal that individuals who regularly practice meditation exhibit a swifter recuperation rate compared to those who do not engage in meditation. Furthermore, meditators demonstrate a greater capacity to effectively manage and adjust to the surrounding circumstances.

Meditation and the brain

Furthermore, the impact of meditation on the mind is even more intriguing, although in this domain, our reliance on personal narratives and observations surpasses the availability of scientific evidence. Nevertheless, the broad trends in brain function can be assessed, though relatively imprecisely, using a device known as an electroencephalograph (EEG). Research conducted employing this instrument reveals discernible patterns of neural activity during meditation that exhibit marked divergence from the typical patterns observed during wakefulness or sleep.

The electroencephalograph is utilized to quantify electric currents within the brain by positioning electrodes on the scalp, establishing a correlation with various mental states. Brainwave activity is categorized into alpha, beta, delta, or theta activity based on the frequency of the electrical patterns that are detected and recorded. The frequency of delta activity ranges from 0.5 to 4 cycles per second, representing the lowest rate, and is primarily correlated with the state of deep sleep. Theta activity is characterized by oscillating patterns occurring at a frequency ranging from 4 to 8 cycles per second. It is associated with states of drowsiness, daydreaming, or the dream state. The primary focus of attention lies on alpha activity, which varies between 8 to 13 cycles per second and prevails when an individual is in a state of relaxation and heightened awareness. The majority of individuals possess the capability to transition from a state of heightened arousal to a state characterized by dominant alpha brain-wave activity merely through the act of shutting their eyes and embracing relaxation. However, it is rather atypical to sustain a state of predominant alpha brain waves with the eyes remaining open. During the state of normal wakefulness, beta activity emerges as the predominant rhythm, oscillating between 13 to approximately 30 or 40 cycles per second.

Alpha activity consistently manifests in meditators across various studies, either independently or in conjunction with other patterns of brain-wave activity;

however, diverse measurements have been recorded across these different studies. There is a high probability that these variations are contingent upon the duration of meditation practice among individuals and the specific modality of meditation employed. The general picture that seems to emerge is that initially, on beginning a period of meditation, there is a shift towards more alpha activity. Subsequently during the practice of meditation, there may arise theta activity, particularly among seasoned practitioners. In the midst of profound meditation, though, intermittent surges of exceedingly elevated beta activity can be observed, ranging from 20 to 40 cycles per second, and occasionally peaking at frequencies as high as 50 cycles per second. Following the conclusion of meditation, the reemergence of alpha activity occurs, which may endure despite the act of opening one's eyes.

An additional intriguing aspect is the observation that the distribution of alpha brain-wave activity during meditation differs from the typical pattern observed throughout the entire scalp. Specifically, it originates from the posterior region of the brain, with the left hemisphere exhibiting initial alpha build-up, followed by the right hemisphere, ultimately resulting in a symmetrical pattern. This is in stark opposition to the typical behavioral patterns exhibited by the majority of individuals. Currently, it is a widely acknowledged fact that the human brain is stratified into two distinct hemispheres, each characterized by its own unique set of cognitive functions. Specifically, the left hemisphere is primarily associated with language processing, analytical reasoning, and related cognitive processes. Conversely, the right hemisphere is predominantly responsible for visual perception, pattern recognition, creative ideation, and similar cognitive functions.

Throughout Western society, there has been a prevailing inclination to attribute greater significance to rational thought, which has consequently led to the prevalence of left hemisphere brain-wave activity in the majority of individuals. This is in juxtaposition with individuals who possess a proclivity towards artistic inclinations, as they typically exhibit predominately right-hemispheric cerebral activity. Despite the current lack of comprehensive understanding regarding the discoveries pertaining to the brain-wave patterns exhibited by practitioners of meditation, it seems evident that meditation has the capacity to redress the equilibrium between the hemispheres of the brain, whilst simultaneously expanding the depth and breadth of brain function into formerly inactive regions.

The Role Of Meditation In Mitigating Pain And Alleviating Symptoms Of Depression

Rarely do individuals instinctively react to pain by exclaiming, "Marvelous!" Undoubtedly, experiencing pain is not a favorable circumstance. Undoubtedly, you desire to actively intervene in order to halt this, yet regrettably, every course of action you undertake appears to bring about unintended harm.

How Pain Works

When the cerebral cortex perceives a potential danger to the physical well-being, it transmits a cautionary signal by means of the sensation of pain. In some peculiar manner, pain serves as a form of safeguarding. It is the innate response of the mind and body to prompt one to step back from impending peril. For example, how do you respond in the event that your hand unexpectedly comes into contact with a scorching stove? You experience a sensation of discomfort and promptly withdraw your hand from the source.

In certain instances, the sensation of pain can endure despite the physical recovery following an injury. The significantly attentive brain faces increased vulnerability when subjected to concerns regarding pain. You harbor apprehensions regarding the possible recurrence of pain, fret over the prospect of adverse developments, experience distress concerning enduring chronic pain, and are rendered immobilized by the overwhelming dread of suffering. These phenomena are commonly referred to as "cognitive contagions" and possess sufficient potency to impede the transmission of nociceptive signals by the delicate neuronal networks of the brain. It engenders an insidious loop of trepidation, distress, angst, and further affliction.

It is now apparent that our thought processes have a direct impact on our perception of pain. The practice of meditation exerts an influence on our cognitive processes, consequently, yielding a substantial impact on our perception of pain. Through the practice of meditation, individuals can acquire the ability to reframe their experience of pain in a manner that diverges from those who do not engage in this contemplative discipline.

The Alleviating Effects of Meditation on Pain Perception

What is the significant disparity? Individuals who engage in the practice of meditation exhibit a heightened level of attentiveness towards the precise physiological experience of discomfort. In experiments involving the administration of painful stimulation, individuals who engage in meditation exhibit heightened levels of neural activity in regions associated with the processing of sensory information. Conversely, individuals who do not engage in meditation exhibit elevated levels of brain activity in regions associated with linguistic processing and critical analysis. The internal monologue expresses, "This is painful! I seem to be quite clumsy. I wonder when this will cease?"

Meditation imparts the brain with the capacity to direct its attention towards the present instant, rather than dwelling on either past occurrences or future prospects. By maintaining mindfulness, you can assuage your vigilant mind even in the absence of immediate threats. In the absence of any discernible threats, the alarm system can cease transmission of distress signals. Your cognitive faculties can allocate a reduced amount of time towards anticipating future unfavorable occurrences.

Meditation appears to alter cerebral rhythms that govern the brain's filtering and processing of diverse sensations, encompassing bodily pain and distressing recollections. It is noteworthy that as a meditator's attention becomes increasingly focused on the sensation of pain and their level of evaluation decreases, their capacity to withstand pain increases. This is a message that is frequently imparted by meditation instructors: Direct your attention towards the sensations and let go of the narrative. It is the narrative that transforms agony into enduring distress.

Furthermore, meditation serves to mitigate pain by relieving symptoms of depression. Depression impedes the brain's capacity to regulate emotions linked to pain. Rather than being a consequence of pain, a melancholic state can actually exacerbate the severity of the pain. The tranquility and equilibrium that accompany the practice of meditation offer relief from depression, consequently reducing suffering.

The practice of meditation and other exercises that involve the integration of mind and body have a lengthy historical background in terms of alleviating pain. Nevertheless, it is in the present moment that scientists are substantiating the effectiveness of these methodologies and attaining a significantly enhanced comprehension of their mechanisms.

An Analysis Of The Desired Future Outlook

Developing a captivating vision for the desired future might seem like an impractical and fanciful utilization of time, but it is, in fact, one of the most efficacious approaches in realizing the aspirations you hold for your life. Developing a perspective for your life may appear to be an impractical and imaginative expenditure of time, yet it holds substantial significance. Reflect upon the notion of a life vision as a guiding instrument that steers you towards optimal courses of action and choices, ultimately propelling you towards the realization of an existence aligned with your desired ideals. This could potentially be regarded as the most beneficial approach for considering the notion of a life vision.

The Essential Need for Having a Vision

Acclaimed authorities and tangible examples of triumph substantiate the concept that possessing a definitive foresight for one's future significantly enhances the likelihood of attaining accomplishments that would otherwise be unfeasible without said vision. Regard the undertaking of formulating your life vision as the act of crafting a detailed visual representation to guide you towards the realization of your personal and professional aspirations. Attaining personal satisfaction and a sense of contentment in life is within one's grasp. Regrettably, it must be acknowledged that failure to foster one's own personal vision will result in relinquishing control to external forces and individuals, ultimately determining the trajectory of one's life.

Crafting a Blueprint for Manifesting Your Ideal Future

Having an immediate, well-defined vision is an unrealistic expectation as it requires ample time and introspection to truly envision one's life and determine the path that will be taken. In addition to fostering vision and perspective, it is imperative to employ rationality and strategic thinking to effectively implement your vision. Your aspirations and ambitions serve as the catalysts for nurturing a formidable vision of excellence. It will engender a sense of vibrancy and zeal, and it will harmonize with your principles and convictions, all of which will bolster your dedication to delving into the potentialities of your existence.

What is it that you seek?

While the question may appear deceptively simple at first glance, formulating a suitable response often proves to be incredibly difficult. Granting oneself the liberty to explore one's deepest desires can elicit significant apprehension. You may also hold the belief that you currently lack the inclination to ponder upon matters as fantastical as your aspirations in life; nonetheless, it is crucial to recall that a life of contentment typically does not manifest fortuitously, but rather by intentional planning and deliberation.

When endeavoring to ascertain your desired aspirations in life, it could prove beneficial to pose inquiries that demand contemplation for formulating an answer. Consider every aspect of your existence, encompassing both tangible and intangible elements, spanning across your professional and personal realms. Consider the myriad of significant elements encapsulating your existence; embrace the profound bonds of kinship and companionship, navigate the trajectory of your professional endeavors, ascertain achievements of unparalleled magnitude, prioritize the preservation of holistic well-being and a heightened standard of living, foster a profound spiritual equilibrium, nurture personal growth, all while indulging in the pursuit of joy and the appreciation of life's pleasures.

"Here are a few suggestions to assist you:

- It is vital to consistently question the underlying reasons for one's desires.
- Direct your attention towards your desired objectives instead of dwelling on unfavorable outcomes.
- Kindly allow yourself the privilege of engaging in contemplative reverie. • Give yourself consent to luxuriate in the realm of fanciful daydreams. • Permit yourself the liberty to indulge in the solace of imaginative musings. • Affirm your right

to immerse yourself in the realm of idyllic reveries.

- Use your imagination. Reflect upon concepts that would have been beyond the realm of your imagination.
- Maintain a focus on your personal objectives rather than conforming to external pressures.

Here are a few inquiries to initiate your investigation:

- In your personal journey, what do you perceive as the utmost essential aspect of existence? What is important is not what should be of concern, but rather what is of actual significance.
- In which domain of your life do you believe there is scope for enhancement?
- Temporarily set aside the matter of finances and ponder what you aspire to achieve in your career.
- What are your most profound aspirations and undisclosed fervors?
- What are certain factors that have the potential to greatly enhance the overall level of joy and happiness in your life?
- What types of interpersonal connections do you aspire to foster throughout your life?

- Of the qualities you presently possess, which one do you desire to enhance the most?
- What are your fundamental principles and beliefs?
- Can you share some of your fundamental convictions and values?
- What are the key tenets that underpin your belief system? What are the matters that concern you?
- What are a few of your proficiencies?
- What are some areas in which you excel?
- Could you please elaborate on your skill set?
- May I inquire about your areas of expertise? What sets you apart from others?
- If you were granted the opportunity to accomplish any pursuit in the world, what would it be?
- What type of enduring heritage would you desire to establish for the succeeding cohorts?

For individuals who derive satisfaction from engaging in creative endeavors, it would be advantageous to maintain a journal or cultivate a vision board as effective instruments for structuring one's thoughts. Engage in personal exploration and seek input from others regarding their aspirations and ambitions in life. Please remain calm and endeavor to infuse this exercise session with an enjoyable atmosphere. It could be advantageous to set aside your responses temporarily and revisit them in the future to examine if any of them have undergone any changes or if you have any additional insights to offer.

An Analysis Of The Distinctions Between Hypnosis And Relaxation Techniques

Comparative Analysis of Relaxation and Self-Hypnosis

B

Both require the attainment of an alternated state of consciousness, wherein the brain transitions from beta wave activity to the slower frequencies associated with alpha levels.

The two are associated with a form of disconnection. Diminish your attentiveness towards the external surroundings and the physical realm, and foster deeper introspection. This engenders a greater sense of mindfulness regarding one's innermost sentiments, cognitions, and affective experiences.

Both necessitate a state of focused attention or concentration. In the practice of meditation, potential focal points may include one's breath, a specific object, a mantra, or an audio recording. For the practice of self-hypnosis, one can utilize the recommendations provided by the hypnotherapist or refer to a pre-recorded session specifically tailored for self-hypnosis.

The Distinction between Relaxation and Hypnosis

This inquiry seems deceptively simple at first glance; however, upon closer examination, it becomes apparent that the abundance of diverse techniques encompassed within the two categories renders it arduous to undertake anything beyond a broad comparison. While there is a lack of clarity in defining the demarcation between meditation and self-hypnosis, I believe it is conceivable to discern a distinction.

In the realm of hypnosis, be it self-induced or facilitated by another individual, there exists a deliberate and purposeful endeavor to access a particular compartment of one's psyche. For instance, when employed within a therapeutic context, hypnosis endeavours to delve into unexposed or suppressed subconscious recollections while directing the individual's focus. It enables the individual to surmount the challenges. Hypnosis can also be employed for the purpose of inducing a positive mental state through the repetition of designated phrases referred to as "affirmative statements." These statements facilitate the subliminal modification by consistently implanting the idea into the conscious mind and allowing it to gradually permeate the subconscious, which serves as the underlying cause of the issue at hand and the gateway to its resolutions.

Hypnotherapy typically emphasizes a more precise result. It may encompass endeavors such as weight reduction, smoking cessation, phobia eradication, among other objectives. At the onset of a hypnotherapy session, employing meditation techniques can effectively pacify the cognitive aspect of the mind. When the ceaseless dialogues of the conscious mind come to an end, they can impart endorsed therapeutic suggestions to the subconscious. Hence, the proposal aims to attain a distinct therapeutic goal. Hypnotherapy is primarily centered on achieving a specific therapeutic outcome.

In contrast, meditation is intended to facilitate the concentration and alignment of one's thoughts, with the objective of directing them towards emptiness. Indeed, I refrained from uttering any words as it remains an arduous task for our cognitive faculties to execute. Apart from times of slumber or lack of consciousness, our waking hours are consumed by thoughts of which we remain oblivious. Once you assume a contemplative stance and endeavor to introspect, do you grasp the challenging nature of this endeavor? It would be advantageous if you possessed precise methodologies to attain a mental state in which you do not consciously contemplate any specific matter.

Conventional meditation typically exhibits a relatively lower degree of organization. Meditation is frequently characterized as the state of mind where thoughts are completely absent. During the practice of meditation, the goal is to achieve a serene state of being by refraining from engaging in conscious mental chatter. During the practice of meditation, it is necessary to devise means to eliminate the manifestation of verbalized conscious thoughts. Meditation is the practice of attaining inner tranquility by embracing one's true self and aligning one's actions in harmony.

The fulfillment of external or internal expectations induces stress. Nevertheless, the practice of meditation has the ability to liberate the mind from such detrimental thoughts and emotions, facilitating a profound sense of tranquility within oneself. During the practice of meditation, our objective is to cultivate a tranquil and undisturbed state of consciousness, devoid of any active cognitions or conscious distractions.

A session of hypnosis or meditation can induce a profound sense of relaxation and enable guided imagery in a serene and peaceful beach setting. Nevertheless, during a hypnosis session, this mental state will be utilized to propose an effective alteration within the depths of the subconscious psyche. An individual who engages in meditation derives advantages from the serenity and respite they encounter. The attainment of tranquility can usher in a state of enlightenment and self-enhancement, bolstering the holistic state of the mind.

The practices of hypnosis and meditation have the ability to induce profound states of relaxation. Both can lay claim to a plethora of comparable health advantages, yet the identical routes to attainment exhibit slight deviations. From this perspective, self-hypnosis can be characterized as an active practice, in contrast to the passive nature inherent in meditation. Using self-hypnosis allows individuals to initiate transformation, whereas meditation enables individuals to facilitate adjustments by stepping aside.

Both methods are highly efficient in fostering personal growth, albeit through distinct approaches. Both possess a level of simplicity and ease of acquisition.

What 5-Minute Meditations Are

Having observed the remarkable advantages derived from brief five minute meditation intervals, let us now delve into a comprehensive examination of this practice. By doing so, we aim to gain a deeper understanding of its simplicity and feasibility for integration into our daily routines, with the ultimate goal of enhancing our lives.

Fundamentals of Five-Minute Meditation

Prior to delving into the assortment of meditation techniques that can be effectively integrated into our daily routines, garnering a transformative impact, it would be prudent to initially acquaint ourselves with the fundamental principles underlying this practice. By gaining a comprehensive understanding of these essentials, we can proficiently execute the techniques in their purest form."

Breathing

Proper breathing constitutes the quintessential initial stage in any form of meditation, and this principle holds true for the five-minute meditation methods you are about to engage in. One simply needs to locate a tranquil and cozy setting in which one may engage in the practice of this exceedingly straightforward yet immensely powerful technique that is employed during meditation. It is imperative to bear in mind the importance of maintaining an upright posture to avoid potential drowsiness or lethargy during the course of the activity.

Now that you have assumed a relaxed posture, it is essential that you direct your attention towards the inhalation and exhalation of your breath through your nasal passages. Direct your attention solely to the sensation of this breath without making any attempt to manipulate or regulate it in any manner. Observe the emergence of thoughts in your mind during any activity, and diligently redirect your focus back to your breath. This will foster the realization that the human mind is inherently subject to straying; nevertheless, one possesses the means to restore it to a state devoid of contemplation.

Mindfulness

It may be surprising, but one has the potential to engage in a form of meditation regardless of their location by integrating mindfulness into their daily existence. Could you kindly provide a precise explanation of the concept of mindfulness?

Mindfulness, in its fundamental nature, entails attaining a cognitive state wherein one directs conscious attention towards the present moment, while simultaneously embracing and acknowledging one's emotions, thoughts, and physical sensations. It is deemed one of the most effective therapeutic instruments within the sphere of meditation.

When individuals embrace the concept of 'mindfulness' in their existence, they naturally gravitate towards being anchored in the 'present moment', steering clear of the tendency of their minds to stray into past reminiscences or future projections, as is customary. Additionally, it affords us the opportunity to encounter experiences with utmost impartiality. Hence, individuals who cultivate mindfulness refrain from labeling their experiences as inherently positive or negative when they encounter them. Simultaneously, we possess an inherent consciousness of the qualitative nature of this encounter, discerning between its positive and negative aspects. Despite this awareness, we deliberately refrain from responding, fostering a state of mental tranquility that is indispensable in attaining inner harmony in the Zen tradition.

The fundamental concept of mindfulness entails engaging in a state of conscious and deliberate awareness towards one's actions. To illustrate, it necessitates more than a general acknowledgement of eating, but rather immersing oneself in the deliberate act of savoring each bite, actively observing and appreciating the texture and flavor of the food, all while purposefully chewing slowly, with the objective being to foster a state of mindfulness. The practice of 'sustaining present awareness' is an incredibly potent approach, particularly in terms of purging the mind and liberating it from the ceaseless influx of superfluous distractions that perennially pervade it.

Focus

The significance of maintaining one's focus should not be underestimated when engaging in a five-minute meditation practice. It is essential to bear in mind that the duration of these meditations should not exceed five minutes. Consequently, there arises a growing imperative to uphold a heightened level of concentration in order to achieve optimal meditation outcomes. You may discover numerous instances in which you are prone to becoming 'distracted' while meditating. A highly effective approach to maintaining optimal focus entails eliminating any potential disturbances that may arise. As an example, it is essential to ensure that your mobile device is placed on silent mode for a duration of five minutes. Failure to do so may disrupt your meditation practice and potentially erase any significant progress you have achieved.

Methods to initiate the preparatory steps for engaging in brief five-minute meditation sessions.

Thus, you are prepared to commence integrating the potency of the aforementioned five minute meditation practices that we will embark upon elaborating on, commencing with the subsequent chapter, correct? Prior to proceeding, it is imperative to comprehend the necessity of adequately equipping oneself prior to embarking on the same endeavor. Now, let us delve into the essential components required to ensure that those brief five-minute meditations have a significant impact.

Allocate a specific space for the purpose of meditation. If you intend to engage in meditation at home, it would be highly desirable to have a dedicated room specifically for this purpose. This room will facilitate adherence to your meditation routine, as it will serve as a perpetual prompt for you to engage in regular meditation sessions, fostering a pervasive sense of tranquility whenever you enter the room.

Acquire appropriate pillows or cushions. If you intend to engage in seated meditation, it is imperative to procure appropriate pillows or cushions to mitigate any discomfort associated with extended periods of sitting, irrespective of duration. It is highly recommended to attain a state of optimal comfort during the practice of meditation, as this can significantly augment the overall quality of the meditative experience.

Get some good incense. You may consider acquiring top-quality incense to enhance the efficacy of your meditation practice. Prior to settling on a specific fragrance that best suits your meditative requirements, it is advisable to experiment with a selection of aromas. You may want to contemplate incorporating lavender into your practice, as its calming aroma can greatly enhance your meditation experience.

Find the time. Many individuals encounter difficulty in allocating sufficient time for their meditative practice. While it may seem feasible to occasionally dedicate a few minutes to meditation, it is inadequate, as regularity is essential. It is imperative, therefore, that you establish fixed intervals throughout the day to engage in meditation. If you choose to meditate at home, it is advisable to allocate the early morning hours and the late evening hours for this purpose. Conversely, if you prefer to meditate at your workplace, you might consider utilizing your lunch hour or even taking advantage of your tea break, which would otherwise be spent socializing with colleagues.

Establishing the ambience through appropriate musical selections. Certain individuals may find it progressively challenging and somewhat monotonous to simply assume a seated position on the floor in order to engage in meditation. Consequently, it can prove highly beneficial to acquire appropriate tranquil music that can be utilized as a background accompaniment during meditation sessions. Naturally, one may desire a portable CD player that offers the convenience of portability, allowing for the enjoyment of tranquil music while engaging in office activities.

Tranquil visual representations, flickering candles and delicate blossoms. You desire to engage in various supplementary activities that aim to enhance your contemplative routine. Although you may prefer not to use scented candles in your workplace, it is entirely acceptable to have serene imagery, such as rainforests or beaches, displayed on your office desk. This will enable you to achieve a profound state of relaxation during meditation. The inclusion of scented candles will contribute to the fragrant ambiance, just as the presence of incense and flowers accomplishes the same effect (in addition to being visually charming).

Sigmund Freud, a prominent figure in the field of psychology, from 1856 to 1939, is widely recognized and highly regarded for his significant contributions and profound impact on the discipline. He was an Australian neurologist who demonstrated a keen interest in patients afflicted with neurosis and hysteria. Hysteria was the designated diagnosis for certain conditions predominantly exhibited by women, characterized by a combination of physical symptoms and emotional disturbances, that seemingly lacked an identifiable physiological basis.

Freud postulated that the origins of most of these conditions stemmed from the realm of the unconscious, contending that the unconscious mind harbored a multitude of impulses and emotions of which an individual remains unaware. By means of this argument, it can be inferred that the examination of behavior and the resolution of patients' difficulties necessitated the ability to delve into the depths of their subconscious mind.

Gaining access to the unconscious mind can solely be achieved through the means of dream analysis, the careful scrutiny of inadvertent verbal slips, and an investigation into the initial expressions uttered by an individual. Consequently, this gave rise to the emergence of psychoanalytic theory, which centers on the significance of the unconscious mind and childhood experiences. As a result, this viewpoint exerted predominant influence over the field of clinical psychology over an extended period.

Sigmund Freud's propositions have been pivotal not only in the discipline of psychology but also in the domains of personality, therapy, and lifespan development. Additionally, Freud postulated the notion that the motivations of adults are shaped by their experiences during childhood, and that both the conscious and unconscious mind hold equal significance in determining an individual's behavior. Contemporary psychotherapeutic approaches have also drawn inspiration from Freudian principles in their examination of how the subconscious mind shapes diverse facets of the individual and interpersonal dynamics, particularly within the therapist-client alliance.

Koffka, Wertheimer, and Kohler are significant contributors in the field of Gestalt Psychology.

Kurt Koffka, Max Wertheimer, and Wolfgang Kohler, all German emigrants, sought refuge in the United States during the early 20th century in order to evade persecution by the Nazis. The three individuals deserve recognition for their role in acquainting American psychologists with the fundamental principles of Gestalt. The term 'Gestalt' inherently denotes 'completeness'. Hence, Gestalt psychology accentuates the notion that a sensory encounter can be deconstructed into discrete components, which, when viewed collectively, establish a cohesive entity. It is this fused totality that governs human perception.

Allow us to examine an illustration. In the context of an orchestral arrangement, a musical composition is typically characterized by a multitude of individual notes, which are then performed by diverse instrumentalists participating in the ensemble. Nevertheless, the full composition and its essential essence can only be apprehended when the individual notes are harmoniously united to create a cohesive interplay of rhythm, melody, and harmony. This notion exhibits a fundamental opposition to the principles of Wundt's structuralism.

Regrettably, upon their entry into the United States, the three individuals were compelled to relinquish their efforts and were consequently unable to continue their research. The burgeoning favor for behaviorism, coupled with the aforementioned factors, curtailed the influential capacity of the Gestalt principles in the United States, in contrast to their prominence in Germany.

Notwithstanding the setbacks, the principles of Gestalt remain pervasive in contemporary times. Psychologists have embraced the viewpoint of regarding a person as a distinct entity rather than as a composite of individually quantified elements, a perspective that has served as the underpinning for numerous humanistic theories, persisting well into recent times. Moreover, these concepts have exerted significant influence on the investigation carried out in the realm of perception and sensation.

It is evident that the doctrines of Freud, Wundt's structuralism, and Gestalt psychology are centered upon the explication and comprehension of internal perceptions. Nevertheless, additional psychologists have articulated apprehensions regarding the possibility of scrutinizing the subjective inner experience within the realm of scientific investigation. Instead, they have opted to concentrate on behavior, as it primarily encompasses the observable manifestations resulting from the underlying cognitive processes.

Pavlov, Skinner, and Watson are prominent figures in the field of Behaviorism.

Furthermore, Russian physiologist Ivan Pavlov remarkably carried out extensive research in the domain of behavior. Specifically, he focuses his research on a cognitive phenomenon known as conditioned reflex, wherein a human being or an animal involuntarily generates a reflexive response to a stimulus. Over time, this response becomes conditioned to occur in response to a separate stimulus that is linked to the original stimulus.

Pavlov examined the phenomenon of an individual exhibiting salivation when exposed to a setting containing nourishment. However, the salivation reflex could still be elicited by an alternative stimulus, such as a distinct auditory cue that is consistently paired with the presence of food, as initially presented in the primary stimulus on multiple occasions. After acquiring the conditioned response to the second stimulus, the initial stimulus, namely the food, is eradicated. This phenomenon is commonly referred to as classical conditioning. Numerous behaviorists have embraced this idea as a means of acquiring behavioral knowledge.

B. F. Skinner was an eminent scholar in the field of psychology, specifically specializing in the study of human behavior and its underlying principles. He hailed from the United States and made significant contributions to the field as a renowned behaviorist. His research centered on the impact that outcomes have on behavior. He discussed punishment and reinforcement as the two prevailing motivating factors. In his scholarly inquiry, he established a controlled environment designed for the meticulous examination of the fundamental principles that dictate the alteration of behavior, employing either punitive measures or rewards. This particular enclosure was referred to as the operant conditioning chamber, whilst it was also commonly known as the Skinner box. This box continues to serve as a crucial research asset that facilitates the examination of behavior.

The Skinner box functions proficiently in sequestering the subject from the surrounding milieu, employing either a button or a lever for behavior discernment. When the subject of investigation activates the button or lever, the apparatus dispenses a form of favorable reinforcement, retribution, or token conditioning that corresponds to either the retribution or the favorable reinforcement.

Furthermore, it is of utmost significance to note that Skinner's emphasis on the implementation of negative and positive reinforcement for learned behavior has had an enduring impact on the field of psychology, particularly due to the subsequent surge in cognitive psychology investigations. However, despite this circumstance, conditioned learning continues to be extensively employed for the purpose of human behavioral modification. In addition, Skinner authored two literary works wherein he expounded upon the significance of operant conditioning as a means to augment bliss and contentment in one's existence. These books have remained notable for presenting highly stimulating propositions pertaining to his methodology.

John B. Additionally, Watson was an esteemed American psychologist who made a substantial impact on the field of psychology during the early 20th century, throughout his tenure at John Hopkins University. Watson held a contrasting viewpoint to James and Wundt's consciousness approach, as he maintained that studying the mind in an objective manner was an insurmountable task. On the contrary, he opted to direct his attention towards observable behavior, and subsequently strive to regulate said behavior for his research. His conviction prompted him to emerge as a foremost advocate for the redirection of psychological scholarship towards behavior, instead of the mind. This methodology of placing emphasis on behavioral aspects is commonly referred to as behaviorism.

A key area of focus for behaviorists lies in the examination of the interplay between acquired behavior and innate attributes. Behaviorists frequently employed animals in their research, operating under the presumption that the observations made on animal subjects could be largely extrapolated to human beings.

Ever since that time, behaviorism has exerted a pervasive influence on the field of experimental psychology for an extended period, and its discoveries continue to hold significant relevance in contemporary times. It has played a crucial role in the establishment of psychology as an independent field of study, particularly through the application of experimental methods and the pursuit of objectivity. Furthermore, it is employed in the context of cognitive-behavioral and behavioral therapy. Behavior modification is extensively employed in classrooms as well. In conclusion, behaviorism is employed in scientific inquiry to examine the interplay between human conduct and stimuli present in the environment.

Strategies for attaining successful outcomes through meditation

Establishing a Purpose through the Practice of Meditation:

What aspirations or goals do you seek to fulfill through the practice of meditation?

It is essential to determine your objectives for engaging in meditation as it significantly influences your motivation to develop a meditation practice and yield favorable outcomes. You may have reservations about engaging in mediation due to the purported health benefits associated with it.

How to Determine Your Objectives in the Practice of Meditation?

Take a moment to observe the deficiencies present within your current circumstances. Examine the issues that you aspire to address and subsequently determine the specific form of meditation that best suits your needs, or explore methods of implementing meditation practices to effectively resolve your concerns or facilitate the attainment of your objectives.

If enhancing your concentration is your objective, focused meditation is the most suitable method for you. If you find it difficult to forgive, it may be beneficial to engage in the practice of loving-kindness meditation. To ascertain your predicament or objective and subsequently seek the optimal method of practice tailored to your needs.

Discern the underlying issue derived from your introspective practice:

Novice practitioners often encounter numerous challenges and setbacks while engaging in meditation, consequently hindering the development of a regular practice. As a result, meditation may be perceived as arduous or uninteresting.

How to Identify these Problems?

One can discern these issues by observing the discomfort experienced during meditation. One may contemplate the factors which render the cultivation of meditation as a habitual practice arduous or unattainable. Then look for solutions. Perhaps you are inadvertently engaging in incorrect methods or lacking the requisite dedication and self-discipline in your approach to your practice.

Do not approach it with excessive seriousness:

The act of engaging in meditation is motivated by the pursuit of important aims such as enhanced concentration or heightened happiness, or it may be sought in order to alleviate weighty concerns such as depression or anxiety. Consequently, meditation is regarded by many individuals as a solemn endeavor. The issue lies in the fact that individuals equate meditation with pharmaceutical medication.

While meditation is typically employed for addressing profound issues, it is important not to approach it with undue seriousness as this will only hinder the inherent benefits and undermine its intended purpose. Suppose one ought to approach meditation as a form of repose. Indeed, it serves as a means of unwinding on a daily basis.

Engage in introspective dialogue:

The primary recipient of the benefits yielded by meditation is your inner self, and I am aware of the challenges that can arise when attempting to comprehend one's inner self.

How to Gain Insight into the Depths of Your Inner Being?

Contemplate the desires of your inner being, or consider the aspirations of your mind. Additionally, consider the items or circumstances that you find undesirable and wish to eliminate. Subsequently, explore the resolution through the identification and adoption of a meditation technique that aligns with your personal preferences and needs. Furthermore, it is important to consider the difficulties that arise during meditation, such as the inability to sustain focus or the feeling of boredom.

How to Engage in Self-Dialogue?

Before you meditate you can talk to yourself in front of the mirror, and ask yourself the things that you want to achieve from meditation, and more importantly try to motivate yourself for doing the things that you find hard during meditation like the concentration on breathing. Alternatively, one could choose to shut their eyes and engage in introspective dialogue with their inner being. I also advise engaging in dialogue with a higher power, and beseeching divine assistance in navigating your spiritual odyssey.

Adopting a healthy eating regimen: "

One's dietary choices significantly influence both their physical and mental well-being, contributing discernibly to their spirituality and overall psychological state. Abstain from the consumption of unhealthy food as it can be a contributing factor to the development of depression and anxiety.

Consuming organic food is highly beneficial for your overall well-being, as it nourishes both the mind and body, and promotes a deep sense of affinity for organic products. Consuming nutritionally deficient food poses adverse implications on one's mental well-being. Therefore, it is imperative to discontinue the consumption of unhealthy fats and junk food if one has developed an addiction towards such dietary habits.

Enhancing Critical Thinking Skills: A Guide To Amplifying Your Analytical Abilities

To embody true leadership, it is essential to maintain a harmonious equilibrium between rationality and emotion. As a leader, one must demonstrate the ability to make rapid decisions, respond judiciously to potential challenges, and competently resolve such challenges. This is the juncture at which the application of discerning reasoning becomes imperative. Emotional intelligence and critical thinking are closely intertwined. Emotional intelligence and critical thinking are closely linked. Emotional intelligence and critical thinking are interconnected. Emotional intelligence and critical thinking are intricately connected. Emotional intelligence and critical thinking share a strong correlation.

The development of critical thinking originates internally. It facilitates the cultivation of rational, constructive, and intent-driven concepts in effectively addressing a matter. You are also expected to acknowledge and duly consider the perspectives, ideas, and concerns put forth by your team members, with the possibility of integrating them into your proposed concepts. In the realm of critical thinking, it is imperative to engage in the cognitive process with impartiality and the absence of any subjective predispositions or evaluative inclinations. A lucid mindset is instrumental in attaining an efficient resolution, as it affords the absence of self-imposed constraints. In the face of a crisis, it behooves one to dismiss personal emotions and direct attention towards the predicament at hand, along with devising effective strategies to rectify it.

Given your current understanding, it is evident that emotional intelligence entails the identification and understanding of various emotions and their underlying origins. This encompasses the emotions of others, alongside your own. By identifying the underlying cause of the issue and analyzing the factors contributing to the associated emotional response, a more comprehensive understanding will be attained, facilitating the formulation of effective resolutions.

It is crucial for a leader to exercise emotional self-control in order to make impartial decisions. Having a strong sense of self-awareness regarding your emotions, coupled with a keen social awareness of the emotions exhibited by those around you, constitutes a significant aspect of emotional intelligence and critical thinking. Comprehending the correlation between the two will enable you to render judicious, fruitful, and astute choices. Upon acquiring the skill of critical thinking, individuals will commence addressing problematic circumstances with a rational and systematic approach.

When an altercation or vigorous debate emerges, it may be prudent to consider whether the matter at hand holds actual significance or if it is merely a futile expenditure of both your own and the other individual's efforts. Can this issue be resolved without engaging in further disagreement? Might it be possible to redirect the passionate vigor showcased in this argument towards an alternative pursuit? Evaluate the circumstances and exercise discernment in arriving at a well-reasoned conclusion, taking into account the acquired insights regarding the issue at hand and its root causes. What may pose a problem to others may not necessarily present a problem to you.

Take cognizance of your own strengths and weaknesses. If presented with the chance to address an issue, seize it. If you hold a personal stake in this argument, ensure that you delineate the backing and rationale behind it. Your objective is to effectively address all conflicts in a constructive manner through proactive measures, rather than resorting to reactive approaches. Attempt to adopt a perspective that empathetically places yourself in the shoes of the other individual, taking into account the potential challenges they might be encountering during that period. Occasionally, upon envisioning oneself in a comparable circumstance as the aforementioned individual, one may come to the realization that their argument is not as devoid of reason as initially perceived. Exercise discernment when selecting your arguments, as certain matters may ultimately prove unworthy of debate.

The inquiry into the desired outcome of a given situation is undoubtedly the utmost significant aspect of exercising critical thinking. What are your goals or objectives? What outcome do you desire to observe? Determine your desired outcome and base your decision accordingly. When making a decision, it is crucial to take into account the potential ramifications it could have on all parties involved. The most unfavorable course of action is to rectify one issue whilst simultaneously giving rise to another. Irrespective of your intentions, your actions will convey a lack of consideration, leading others to harbor doubts about your future decision-making. If it is inevitable that your decision will have adverse impacts on others, ensure that you provide clear justification for the compelled nature of your decision. Provide them with the guarantee that a significant portion of your decisions will not have a negative impact and that you will devise strategies to capitalize on the given circumstances.

An advisable strategy for engaging in critical thinking is to employ the conventional sequence of "who, what, when, where, why, how." Take, for instance, the scenario where one of your employees engages in conduct that prompts you to raise doubts. Ask yourself:

Who did it?

What did they do?

At what time did they perform the task?

Where was the activity conducted?

What was the motive behind their actions?

What methods did they employ to achieve this outcome, and what measures can I undertake to rectify the situation?

By utilizing this straightforward methodology, you are establishing a systematic approach to comprehensively articulate all pertinent aspects of the matter, identify its fundamental cause, and ultimately achieve its resolution. This approach has the potential to be utilized across a wide range of circumstances. Through adopting a contemplative approach and meticulously examining the matter, you might uncover something that had evaded your notice previously. Taking a temporary hiatus from a situation in which you have direct involvement enables you to evaluate the circumstances with a heightened sense of objectivity.

In order to attain optimal levels of critical thinking proficiency and efficacy:

You should possess the capability to pose significant inquiries in relation to the identification of resolutions for issues.

It is imperative that you possess the capacity to gather and analyze pertinent data that is applicable to the circumstances.

It is essential to approach the problem-solving process with objectivity and an open mind.

In order to resolve the problem, it is imperative that you engage in effective communication with others.

Excluding one's emotions from the process of decision-making forms an integral component of the concept of critical thinking. By adopting this approach, you can achieve impartiality in your decision-making process, leading to enhanced effectiveness. Certain individuals argue that emotional intelligence and critical thinking are unrelated, positing that critical thinking primarily serves as a cognitive instrument. Nevertheless, their perspective neglects the fundamental truth that emotional intelligence encompasses the capacity to disengage emotionally from a situation in order to arrive at a rational and unbiased conclusion.

Emotional intelligence and critical thinking are pertinent to virtually every circumstance we encounter. Irrespective of one's chosen vocation, the imperative to engage in critical thinking remains constant. Within the present era, it is indisputable that knowledge holds significant power. The prosperity of our economy, the stability of our careers, and the trajectory of our personal lives are all contingent upon acquiring comprehensive knowledge and exercising astute judgement in a timely manner. Possessing the necessary skills to accomplish that task is indeed a valuable asset. The possession of impeccable emotional intelligence and an aptitude for astute critical thinking will pave the way for triumph in all facets of your existence.

Critical thinking encourages individuals to engage in more coherent and open-minded thought processes. It facilitates the opportunity for you to articulate your concerns, propose solutions, and present ideas at a heightened level of sophistication. Despite being a cognitive mode of thinking, critical thinking affords individuals the opportunity to manifest their creativity through intellectual means. It is not merely a matter of the concepts you possess, but rather the manner in which you articulate them. Do they bear relevance to the current circumstances? Do they possess efficacy in regard to the resolution of the predicament? That is where the application of critical thinking becomes crucial.

Additionally, it serves as a means for self-assessment. As an illustrative instance, in the event that you encounter a state of distress regarding a matter, you may inquire as to the root cause underlying your emotional state by posing the question, "What is the reason for my current emotional response?" By whom was I made to feel this way? How can I cultivate a sense of emotional well-being in relation to this matter? Posing appropriate inquiries in any given situation is the initial stride towards resolving the issue.

Upon diligent inquiry and meticulous data collection, an individual proficient in critical reasoning will possess the acumen to identify and retain pertinent information while discarding extraneous elements. They will possess the ability to examine the issue comprehensively and render an impartial judgement predicated upon their observations. They will possess the ability to evaluate all the feasible alternatives in a logical manner as well. These are the individuals whom others seek in times of crisis.

A crucial attribute possessed by individuals who engage in critical thinking is the unwavering belief in the choices they make. Given their thorough evaluation of the particulars, evidence and various perspectives pertaining to the matter at hand, they will exhibit unwavering confidence in their decisions without any inclination for self-doubt. Individuals possessing a heightened degree of emotional intelligence tend to rely on their intuition and frequently align their actions with their inner instincts.

www.ingramcontent.com/pod-product-compliance
Lightning Source LLC
Chambersburg PA
CBHW050235120526
44590CB00016B/2094